LIVE IT:
INCLUSIVENESS

MARINA COHEN

Crabtree Publishing Company
www.crabtreebooks.com

Author: Marina Cohen
Coordinating editor: Bonnie Dobkin
Publishing plan research and development:
  Sean Charlebois, Reagan Miller
  Crabtree Publishing Company
Editor: Reagan Miller
Proofreader: Crystal Sikkens
Editorial director: Kathy Middleton
Production coordinator: Margaret Salter
Prepress technician: Margaret Salter

Logo design: Samantha Crabtree
Project Manager: Santosh Vasudevan (Q2AMEDIA)
Art Direction: Rahul Dhiman (Q2AMEDIA)
Design: Neha Kaul (Q2AMEDIA)
Illustrations: Q2AMEDIA
Front Cover: Jason McElwain, a teenager with autism, celebrates
  with his teammates after he scored 20 points in a
  championship game.
Title Page: Students at Charleston High School in Mississippi end
  years of segregation by deciding to have an integrated prom

Library and Archives Canada Cataloguing in Publication

Cohen, Marina
    Live it: inclusiveness / Marina Cohen.

(Crabtree character sketches)
Includes index.
ISBN 978-0-7787-4890-8 (bound).--ISBN 978-0-7787-4923-3 (pbk.)

    1. Respect for persons--Juvenile literature. 2. Social integration--
Juvenile
literature. 3. Biography--Juvenile literature. I. Title. II. Title:
Inclusiveness.
III. Series: Crabtree character sketches

BJ1533.R42C64 2010   j179'.9   C2009-905372-1

Library of Congress Cataloging-in-Publication Data

Cohen, Marina, 1967-
  Live it-- inclusiveness / Marina Cohen.
    p. cm. -- (Crabtree character sketches)
  Includes index.

  ISBN 978-0-7787-4923-3 (pbk. : alk. paper) -- ISBN 978-0-7787-4890
(reinforced library binding : alk. paper)

  1. Respect for persons--Juvenile literature. 2. Social integration--
Juvenile literature. 3. Biography--Juvenile literature. I. Title.

  BJ1533.R42C64 2010
  179'.9--dc22

            2009035501

Crabtree Publishing Company

www.crabtreebooks.com   1-800-387-7650

Printed in the USA/122009/BG20090930

Published in Canada
Crabtree Publishing
616 Welland Ave.
St. Catharines, ON
L2M 5V6

Published in the United States
Crabtree Publishing
PMB 59051
350 Fifth Avenue, 59th Floor
New York, New York 10118

Published in the United Kingdom
Crabtree Publishing
Maritime House
Basin Road North, Hove
BN41 1WR

Published in Austral
Crabtree Publishing
386 Mt. Alexander Rd.
Ascot Vale (Melbourne)
VIC 3032

CONTENTs

INCLUSIVENESS MEANS BEING OPEN TO OTHER PEOPLE'S IDEAS AND BELIEFS. IT MEANS ACCEPTING THOSE WHO ARE DIFFERENT AND MAKING THEM FEEL WELCOME.

WITH THE HELP OF OTHERS, THE PEOPLE ON THESE PAGES WERE ABLE TO BREAK DOWN SOME COMMON *BARRIERS* TO INCLUSION. LET'S TAKE A LOOK AT THEIR STORIES!

JASON MCELWAIN
TEENAGER WITH *AUTISM*

HAYLEY WICKENHEISER
FEMALE HOCKEY PLAYER

4

SENIORS FROM CHARLESTON
HIGH SCHOOL IN MISSISSIPPI

ANGIE GROH
SOPHOMORE WHO TAUGHT COMPUTER
SKILLS TO SENIOR CITIZENS

OSCAR PISTORIUS
ATHLETE WITH ARTIFICIAL LIMBS

TANYA WALTERS
BUS DRIVER WHO FOUNDED
THE GODPARENTS YOUTH ORGANIZATION

INCLUDING THOSE WITH SPECIAL NEED

JASON MCELWAIN

WHO IS HE?
A YOUNG MAN WITH AUTISM

WHY HIM?
HE MADE NATIONAL NEWS WHEN HE PLAYED FOR FOUR MINUTES DURING A HIGH SCHOOL BASKETBALL GAME.

JASON MCELWAIN HAS AUTISM. AUTISM IS A DISORDER THAT MAKES IT DIFFICULT FOR PEOPLE TO COMMUNICATE WITH OTHERS OR TAKE PART IN EVERYDAY ACTIVITIES. BUT ON FEBRUARY 15, 2006 JASON LEARNED WHAT IT FELT LIKE TO BE PART OF A TEAM.

IN HIS JUNIOR YEAR, JASON MCELWAIN TRIED OUT FOR THE BASKETBALL TEAM AT GREECE ATHENA HIG SCHOOL. BUT AT 5'6"*, HE DIDN'T MAKE IT.

I WISH I'D BEEN ABLE TO USE HIM. THE KID LOVES BASKETBALL MORE THAN ANYTHING. THER MUST BE SOME WAY TO GET HIM INVOLVED...

* THAT'S 1.7 METERS FOR METRIC READERS OUT THE

YO! I MADE THE TEAM!

ME TOO, MAN!

GYM OFFICE

HEY LOO JASON— YOU'RE TE MANAGER

6

...CTICE AFTER PRACTICE, SEASON AFTER SEASON, ...ON SHOWED UP TO HELP THE TEAM.

LET'S GO, GUYS! HIT YOUR SHOTS!

THANKS, J-MAC!

...JASON'S SENIOR YEAR, HIS TEAM MADE ...O THE CHAMPIONSHIPS. HIS COACH ...HIM ON THE *ROSTER* FOR THE GAME, ...OMISING TO TRY TO GET HIM IN. THEN, ...H FOUR MINUTES LEFT...

OKAY, WE'VE GOT A BIG LEAD. JASON'S GOING TO PLAY.

10

4:00

ATHENA 74

GUEST 54

AND THE CROWD BEGAN TO *CHANT*

J-MAC! J-MAC! J-MAC!

7

HIS TEAMMATES PASSED THE BALL TO HIM, AND JASON TOOK HIS SHOT.

J-MAC! J-MAC!

AHHHH!

PLEASE, JUST LET HIM GET ONE BASKET.

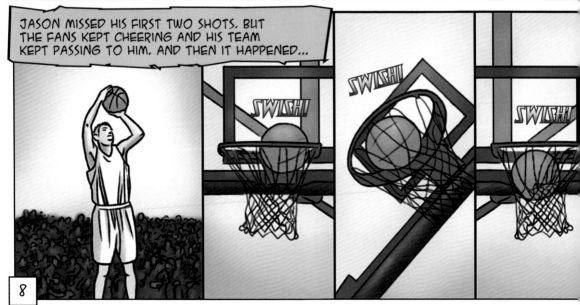

JASON MISSED HIS FIRST TWO SHOTS. BUT THE FANS KEPT CHEERING AND HIS TEAM KEPT PASSING TO HIM. AND THEN IT HAPPENED...

SWISH!

SWISH!

SWISH!

...SON HIT BASKET AFTER ...KET. THE FANS WENT WILD.

WAY TO GO, JASON!

J-MAC TO THE RACK!

WHEN THE BUZZER SOUNDED, ENDING THE GAME, JASON MCELWAIN HAD HIT 6 THREE-POINTERS AND 1 TWO-POINTER FOR A TOTAL OF 20 POINTS IN FOUR MINUTES. GREECE ATHENA HAD A NEW HERO!

BECAUSE HIS COACH AND TEAM WERE WILLING TO INCLUDE HIM, JASON HAD A CHANCE TO DO WHAT HE LOVED. IN TURN, HE SHOWED EVERYONE THAT PEOPLE WHO ARE "DIFFERENT" CAN STILL *ACCOMPLISH* AMAZING THINGS.

WHAT WOULD YOU DO?

ARE THERE ANY KIDS IN YOUR SCHOOL WITH SPECIAL NEEDS? MAYBE THERE ARE STUDENTS WITH AUTISM, DOWN SYNDROME, OR SOME KIND OF PHYSICAL DISABILITY. WHAT CAN YOU DO TO MAKE SURE THEY ARE INCLUDED IN SCHOOL ACTIVITIES? HOW CAN YOU MAKE SURE THEY FEEL VALUED AND RESPECTED?

HAYLEY WICKENHEISER

WHO IS SHE?
A FEMALE HOCKEY PLAYER

WHY HER?
SHE WAS THE FIRST WOMAN TO SCORE A POINT IN A MEN'S PRO LEAGUE.

HOCKEY WAS ONCE THOUGHT TO BE PRETTY MUCH A GUY'S SPORT. BUT THEN A GIRL NAMED HAYLEY WICKENHEISER CAME ALONG, AND SHE PLAYED AS WELL AS ANYONE— AND BETTER THAN MOST.

WOULD THE BOYS INCLUDE HER ON THEIR TEAMS? LET'S FIND OUT.

SHAUNAVON, SASKATCHEWAN. WINTER, 1984.

ONCE THE ICE IS READY I'M GOING TO TEACH YOU HOW TO SKATE...

BUT HAYLEY WASN'T CONTENT WITH JUST SKATING.

CAN YOU TEACH ME HOW TO PLAY HOCKEY, DADDY? I LOVE HOCKEY!

BUT WOULD THE BOYS BE HAPPY ABOUT HAVING A GIRL ON THEIR TEAM?

OUR NEWEST PLAYER'S NAME IS HAYLEY WICKENHEISER. SHE'S A SKILLED SKATER AND HAS A LETHAL SLAP SHOT...

BUT, UM, COACH?

I DON'T WANT TO HEAR IT, PARKER. SHE'S GOOD. REALLY GOOD.

NO, IT'S JUST...WHERE SHE GOING TO CHANGE

IT WASN'T LONG BEFORE HAYLEY GOT NOTICED.

WHO IS THAT GUY? HE'S GOT A CANNON!

IT'S THAT WICKENHEISER KID--HE'S ALREADY SCORED FOUR GOALS.

HE IS A SHE--AND HER NAME IS HAYLEY!

WHEN HAYLEY WAS ONLY 15, SHE JOINED THE CANADIAN WOMEN'S NATIONAL HOCKEY TEAM. ONCE AGAIN, SHE WAS A STAR!

AND THE *MVP* AWARD GOE TO HAYLEY WICKENHEISER.

IN 1998, WOMEN'S HOCKEY BECAME AN OFFICIAL SPORT OF THE WINTER OLYMPICS...

AND THEN, AFTER HER TEAM WON THE SILVER...

HAYLEY WICKENHEISER HAS JUST BEEN NAMED TO THE ALL-STAR TEAM!

I'M BOBBY CLARKE, THE MEN'S TEAM CANADA GENERAL MANAGER. I'D LIKE TO INVITE YOU TO THE PHILADELPHIA FLYERS *ROOKIE* CAMP.

IN **2002**, HAYLEY WAS IN THE OLYMPICS AGAIN. THIS TIME CANADA TOOK THE GOLD, AND HAYLEY, WHO LED THE TEAM IN SCORING, WON MVP.

HAYLEY WAS SUCH AN OUTSTANDING PLAYER THAT IN **2003**, SHE WAS INCLUDED IN A MEN'S PROFESSIONAL LEAGUE. IT SEEMS THAT WHEN EVERYONE'S INCLUDED, EVERYONE BENEFITS!

WHAT WOULD YOU DO?

A BOY WANTS TO JOIN AN ALL-GIRLS' CHEERLEADING SQUAD. HE SEEMS LIKE A GOOD GUY, BUT THERE'S NEVER BEEN A BOY ON THE SQUAD BEFORE.

IF YOU WERE THE SQUAD'S ADVISOR, WHAT WOULD YOU SAY TO THE GIRLS?

CHARLESTON HIGH SCHOOL SENIORS, CLASS OF 2008

WHY THEM?
THEY ATTENDED THE SCHOOL'S FIRST **INTEGRATED PROM.**

MISSISSIPPI SCHOOLS HAD BEEN INTEGRATED SINCE 1970, BUT OLD ATTITUDES **LINGERED.** YEAR AFTER YEAR, CHARLESTON HIGH SCHOOL WOULD HOLD TWO PROMS—ONE FOR WHITE STUDENTS AND THE OTHER FOR AFRICAN-AMERICAN STUDENTS.

WHAT FINALLY MADE THE COMMUNITY REALIZE THAT A SCHOOL PROM SHOULD INCLUDE ALL STUDENTS? THE ANSWER MIGHT SURPRISE YOU.

ACTOR MORGAN FREEMAN, A RESIDENT OF CHARLESTON, HAD MADE AN OFFER TO THE CHARLESTON SCHOOL BOARD WAY BACK IN 1997...

SEPARATE PROMS ARE AN EMBARRASSMENT T[O] OUR COMMUNITY. YOU ALL WILL HAVE [AN] INTEGRATED DANC[E] I'LL PAY FOR THE WHOLE THING!

WE'RE NOT INTERESTED.

IT'S NOT GOING TO HAPPEN.

THE PARENTS DO[N'T] WANT IT, AND TH[E] SCHOOL BOARD SUPPORTS THEM

BUT YEAR AFTER YEAR, EVERYONE REFUSED...

...EN, IN **2008**, CANADIAN ...MMAKER PAUL SALTZMAN HEARD ...UT MR. FREEMAN'S OFFER.

IS THIS TRUE?

YEP. I KEEP OFFERING, AND THEY KEEP SAYING NO.

MAYBE THE ANSWER WOULD BE DIFFERENT IF THEY KNEW THEY COULD BE IN A MOVIE.

MAYBE IT WAS THE MOVIE. MAYBE THE TOWN JUST KNEW IT WAS TIME FOR A CHANGE. BUT WHEN MR. FREEMAN MADE HIS OFFER AGAIN...

THANK YOU, MR. FREEMAN.

I'VE WAITED A LONG TIME FOR THIS.

THIS IS GOING TO BE THE BEST PROM IN THE HISTORY OF CHARLESTON HIGH!

...T EVERYONE ...REED.

...ON'T KNOW ...Y I'M EVEN ...OING TO ...HIS BORING ...LD PROM.

...I DON'T THINK ...'LL BE BORING. I THINK IT'LL BE GREAT!

OR MISERABLE. I MEAN, THINK ABOUT IT. WITH ALL OF US AT ONE PROM... WHAT IF EVERYONE JUST STANDS AROUND AND STARES AT EACH OTHER?

ANOTHER CUSTOMER HEARD THEM.

YOU YOUNG FOLKS HAVE NO IDEA JUST HOW IMPORTANT THIS PROM IS! DO YOU KNOW WHAT SOME OF US *SACRIFICED* TO GET THOSE SCHOOLS OF YOURS INTEGRATED?

HISTORY-MAKING OR NOT, SOME PARENTS WERE STILL AGAINST THE PROM...

I DON'T SEE WHY THEY HAVE TO GO AND HAVE AN INTEGRATED PROM AFTER ALL THESE YEARS. I WISH YOU WEREN'T GOING.

BUT I AM, MOM. THOSE KIDS ARE MY FRIENDS. THIS SHOULD HAVE HAPPENED A LONG TIME AGO.

TO COMPETE WITH THE INTEGRATED PROM A GROU OF WHITE PARENTS ORGAN AN ALL-WHITE PROM.

I'M GLAD MY KID IS GOING TO THE ALL-WHITE PROM WE ORGANIZED.

JUNE 2008--PROM NIGHT.

LOOK AT THIS. WE DID IT. EVEN THOUGH NO ONE THOUGHT IT WOULD EVER HAPPEN.

INCLUDING OLDER PEOPLE

ANGIE GROH

WHO IS SHE?
A HIGH SCHOOL **SOPHOMORE** IN THORNTON, IOWA

WHY HER?
SHE TAUGHT COMPUTER SKILLS TO SENIORS IN HER COMMUNITY.

THE **DIGITAL** DIVIDE IS WHAT SOME PEOPLE CALL THE GAP BETWEEN THOSE WHO HAVE ACCESS TO COMPUTERS AND THOSE WHO DO NOT. BUT IT'S ALSO THE GAP BETWEEN THOSE WHO KNOW HOW TO USE COMPUTERS AND THOSE WHO DON'T.

AT JUST 16 YEARS OLD, ANGIE GROH REALIZED THE GAP IN HER COMMUNITY WAS GROWING. SHE WANTED TO MAKE SURE EVERYONE WAS INCLUDED IN THE WORLD OF TECHNOLOGY.

TEENS TEACHING INTERNET SKILLS **CONFERENCE,** UNIVERSITY OF MARYLAND, **2000**

WHAT GOOD IS A COMPUTER IF YOU DON'T KNOW HOW TO USE IT? THE POOR AND THE ELDERLY ARE BEING LEFT BEHIND IN THIS TECHNOLOGICAL AGE...

I NEVER THOUGHT ABOUT OLDER PEOPLE BEING LEFT BEHIND! IT'S TOO BAD. I BET A LOT OF THEM WOULD LOVE IT.

NOTHING MUCH WE CAN DO ABOUT IT, THOUGH.

MAYBE THERE

ANGIE QUICKLY PUT A
PLAN INTO ACTION.

THERE. NOW LET'S SEE WHO'S INTERESTED

WHAT A WONDERFUL IDEA! I'D LOVE TO LEARN HOW TO SEND THOSE "E-MAIL" THINGS TO MY GRANDCHILDREN.

AND I HEAR YOU CAN READ NEWSPAPERS FROM ANY CITY IN THE WORLD! YOU CAN EVEN MAKE THE PRINT LARGE ENOUGH SO YOU CAN ACTUALLY SEE IT!

PRETTY SOON, ANGIE HAD TEN STUDENTS.

THIS IS PERFECT! NOW I JUST NEED A LOCATION...

SURE, ANGIE. YOU CAN USE THE SCHOOL'S IMAC LAB SATURDAY MORNINGS. GLAD TO HELP!

THORNTON ELEMENTARY MIDDLE SCHOOL

THANKS!

19

ANGIE *RECRUITED* OTHER TEENS FROM HE[R] COMMUNITY AND FROM AS FAR AWAY AS T[H]E NORTH-CENTRAL REGION OF IOWA.

OSCAR PISTORIUS

WHO IS HE?
AN ATHLETE AND
A DOUBLE **AMPUTEE**

WHY HIM?
HE MADE HISTORY AS THE FIRST
PARALYMPIC RUNNER ALLOWED
TO COMPETE INTERNATIONALLY
ALONGSIDE **ABLE-BODIED** RUNNERS.

SOMETIMES, THE ONLY THING THAT STOPS SOMEONE FROM BEING INCLUDED IS ATTITUDE. IT MIGHT BE THE ATTITUDES OF OTHERS. OR, IT COULD BE THE PERSON'S OWN OUTLOOK ON LIFE.

OSCAR PISTORIUS HAD TWO PROSTHETIC LEGS. ANOTHER PERSON IN HIS SITUATION MIGHT NOT HAVE THOUGHT ABOUT BEING AN ATHLETE. BUT WITH THE RIGHT ATTITUDE, ANYTHING IS POSSIBLE!

NOVEMBER 22, 1986, SANDTON, GAUTENG, SOUTH AFRICA...

I'M AFRAID YOUR SON HAS A RARE DEFORMITY. HE'S MISSING BONES BETWEEN HIS KNEES AND HIS ANKLES.

WHEN OSCAR TURNED ONE, HIS PARENTS MADE A HEARTBREAKING DECISION. OSCAR'S LEGS WERE AMPUTATED JUST BELOW THE KNE

WHAT WILL HAPPEN TO HI HENKE? WILL HE EVER FIT WITH OTHER CHILDREN?

HE'LL BE JUST FINE, SHEILA. YOU'LL SEE.

TANYA WALTERS

WHO IS SHE?
A BUS DRIVER FOR THE LOS ANGELES UNIFIED SCHOOL DISTRICT

WHY HER?
SHE TAKES TEENS ON LIFE-CHANGING TRIPS.

VISITING ANOTHER PLACE IS MORE THAN JUST A TRIP. IT'S A CHANCE TO LEARN, GROW, AND EXPLORE. THAT'S WHY SCHOOLS TAKE FIELD TRIPS. THAT'S WHY SOME FAMILIES TRAVEL.

BUT WHAT HAPPENS TO KIDS WHO DON'T GET THIS CHANCE? TANYA WALTERS DECIDED IT WAS TIME SOMEONE INCLUDED LESS *FORTUNATE* KIDS IN THIS KIND OF EXPERIENCE.

EVERY DAY, TANYA WALTERS DROVE HER BUS ROUTE, PICKING UP KIDS AND GETTING TO KNOW THEM.

GOOD MORNING.

YEAH? WHAT'S SO GOOD ABOUT IT?

YOU DON FOOL M I KNOW YOU'RE GOOD K

TANYA LOVED HER JOB. AND THE STUDE WHO RODE HER BUS—EVEN THE ONES W MAJOR ATTITUDE—LOVED HER.

GUESS WHAT MISS TANYA? IN A COUPLE OF WEEKS, I'M GOING ON A TRIP TO VISIT SOME COLLEGES.

WOW—THAT'S GREAT! I BET YOU'RE EXCITED.

TANYA USED THE TRIPS TO TEACH THE STUDENTS VALUABLE LIFE-LESSONS.

AND MAYBE YOU'LL THINK TWICE ABOUT BELONGING TO GANGS THAT GO BEATING PEOPLE UP JUST FOR WEARING RED OR BLUE!

IN SCHOOL, THEY TAUGHT US ABOUT ALL THE SACRIFICES THOSE *CIVIL RIGHTS* LEADERS MADE, BUT I NEVER UNDERSTOOD...

THE WORLD'S LOOKING A WHOLE LOT DIFFERENT NOW.

I GET IT NOW, I REALLY GET IT!

MARTIN LUTHER KING. JR.

BY INCLUDING KIDS IN ROAD TRIPS THEY WOULD NEVER HAVE BEEN ABLE TO TAKE, TANYA WALTERS HAS MADE A DIFFERENCE. HER GODPARENTS YOUTH ORGANIZATION GETS KIDS OFF THE STREETS, AND SEVEN OF HER KIDS HAVE GONE ON TO COLLEGE. SHE HOPES SHE CAN KEEP GIVING KIDS THIS CHANCE.

AS SHE HERSELF SAID, "I JUST WANT THESE KIDS TO BE ABLE TO DREAM."

WHAT WOULD YOU DO?

YOUR CLASS IS GOING ON A SCHOOL TRIP. YOU DISCOVER THAT A FEW STUDENTS IN YOUR CLASS CAN'T GO BECAUSE THEY CAN'T AFFORD IT. WHAT COULD YOU DO TO MAKE SURE THESE STUDENTS ARE INCLUDED?

29

WEB SITES

TO UNDERSTAND MORE ABOUT AUTISM, WHAT IT IS, AND HOW IT AFFECTS PEOPLE, VISIT THIS INFORMATIVE WEB SITE.

kidshealth.org/kid/health_problems/brain/autism.html

FOR MORE INFORMATION ABOUT HOW TANYA WALTERS HAS HELPED YOUNG PEOPLE THROUGH HER ORGANIZATION, CHECK THIS OUT.

www.godparentsclub.org

LEARN ADDITIONAL INTERESTING FACTS AND STATISTICS ABOUT OSCAR PISTORIUS.

www.ossur.com/?PageID=3364

DOES YOUR FAMILY HAVE AN OLD COMPUTER LYING AROUND? LEARN HOW YOU CAN HELP BRIDGE THE DIGITAL DIVIDE.

www.bridgethedigitaldivide.com

ARE YOU INTERESTED IN WOMEN'S HOCKEY? CHECK OUT THIS SITE.

www.owha.on.ca/mainowha.asp

GLOSSARY

ABLE-BODIED HAVING A SOUND, STRONG BODY

ACCOMPLISH TO ACHIEVE A GOAL OR TO CARRY OUT A TASK

AMPUTEE SOMEONE WHO HAS HAD A LIMB AMPUTATED

AUTISM A SOCIAL/COMMUNICATION DISORDER THAT AFFECTS COMMUNICATION AND SOCIALIZATION

BARRIERS THINGS THAT STAND IN THE WAY OF ACHIEVING A GOAL

CHANT TO REPEAT A PHRASE OVER AND OVER

CIVIL RIGHTS THE RIGHTS OF A CITIZEN

CONFERENCE A FORMAL MEETING OR GATHERING FOR THE PURPOSE OF DISCUSSION OR DEBATE

DIGITAL RELATING TO ELECTRONICS, ESPECIALLY COMPUTER TECHNOLOGY

ESSAYS WRITTEN COMPOSITIONS

FIBER A NATURAL OR SYNTHETIC STRAND

FORTUNATE LUCKY

ICON A PICTURE REPRESENTATION

INTEGRATED INCLUDING PEOPLE OF VARIOUS RACIAL, ETHNIC, AND RELIGIOUS GROUPS

LEAGUES ASSOCIATIONS OF SPORTS TEAMS THAT ORGANIZE TOURNAMENTS

LINGERED TO TAKE A LONG TIME TO LEAVE OR DISAPPEAR

MVP ABBREVIATION FOR MOST VALUABLE PLAYER

PARALYMPICS A SERIES OF INTERNATIONAL COMPETITIONS HELD FOR ATHLETES WITH DISABILITIES

PROM A DANCE HELD FOR A GRADUATING CLASS

RECRUITED TO ENROLL OR ENLIST NEW MEMBERS

ROOKIE A PLAYER IN HIS OR HER FIRST YEAR ON A PROFESSIONAL TEAM

ROSTER LIST OF NAMES OF PLAYERS ON A TEAM

SACRIFICED TO GIVE UP SOMETHING VALUABLE IN ORDER TO HELP ANOTHER PERSON

SOPHOMORE A STUDENT IN HIS OR HER SECOND YEAR OF COLLEGE OR HIGH SCHOOL

INDEX